To J[...]

A w[...],

A FELLOW CANCER
        SURVIVOR —

I HOPE YOU ENJOY,
   "THE RAMBLINGS"?

May You ALWAYS BE A
        WINNER
        AND
May You CONTINUE TO —
" Do ONLY THAT, WHICH YOU "
   KNOW TO BE RIGHT!

        Carson Dan

                        7/2008

The Ramblings of a Grandfather!

*Samplings of My
Self-Perceived
Wisdom*

Carson M. Doss

"We often brag about other people to other people, but we seldom brag to the person we are bragging about".

The Ramblings of a Grandfather

Copyright © 2005 Carson M. Doss

Library of Congress
Cataloging-in-Publication Data
ISBN 1-56167-918-6

Library of Congress Card Catalog Number:
2005908147

Published by

American Literary Press
8019 Belair Road, Suite 10
Baltimore, Maryland 21236

Manufactured in the United States of America

These Ramblings were begun on September 15, 2004 after sixty years of observing human nature. They are my own thoughts and beliefs and you may either agree or disagree. I simply am throwing them out and it remains to be seen if they stick.
I hope you enjoy.

These Ramblings are dedicated to my wonderful family that is the center of my life!

A special thank you to my supportive wife who not only encouraged me to put these ramblings into written form, but who also created and recreated, many times, the manuscript for publishing. I also thank her for saying yes to my marriage proposal over thirty-six years ago and for having continually overlooked my frailties, weaknesses, and mistakes for all the years of our wonderful life together. I truly married out of my league.
I love you Peaches!!!

TOPICS

My Philosophical Overview of Life As Told To My Granddaughter

Written to my granddaughter, Lauren Elizabeth Doss, on June 12, 1997 at two weeks of age.

Recorded on a birthday CD for her sixth birthday May 29, 2003

Lauren, I welcome you to life with open arms and an open heart. This note contains some of my thoughts about life and about some of the traits that I believe people should possess.

You are embarking upon your life's adventure that will last many years. The adventure will have sorrow, heartaches, disappointments, and some very difficult times. But, if you remain mentally tough, you must be tough, you will survive all of life's hurdles and have a great deal of fun. An old song teaches that when you have difficult times you should "pick yourself up, dust yourself off, and start all over again". The majority of your adventure will be very rewarding, very fulfilling, and very joyous if you so desire and if you will simply do only that, which you know to be right.

Your loving parents and your church will teach you right from wrong. Your parents and your church will also set the right example from which to pattern your thoughts, traits, and actions. You are very fortunate to have the wonderful parents that you have and I hope as you grow up you will realize just how fortunate you are.

Always, always seek the good in every person, in every situation, and in everything. Sometimes it may be difficult to find the good but if you look hard enough and long enough, you will find the good. Another old song says – "accentuate the positive – eliminate the negative". Having a positive attitude will make your life's adventure much easier.

Treat others as you wish to be treated. What goes around comes around.

Do not hold grudges – and do not allow yourself to become bitter if someone hurts you (and they will).

Never, ever allow someone to control or change your attitudes, your beliefs, your faith, or your destiny.

The world cannot make you cry unless you let it.

You and your faith and only you and your faith have control of your life. You have the intelligence, the ability, and the strength of your faith to create the destiny of your choice.

Lauren, you have my commitment to be available at anytime for anything that I can possibly do for you. Just look for me in the grandstand of life and you will always see me there cheering you on. Always remember that I will come down out of the grandstand anytime you need me.

Just as you will strive to be a better person, I will continue to strive to be the best possible grandfather.

Lauren, I love you and I wish you strength, wisdom, and happiness for the rest of your life.

Granddaddy

Granddaddy

PERSONAL GOALS I

PERSONAL GOALS

When I am gone, I hope it will be said of me, "he was a good man, a good son, a good husband, a good father, a good grandfather, a good in-law, and he gave more than he received."

To be the president of a Fortune 500 company was always my business goal and life long dream. Now that time has begun to become shorter, my dream is no longer viable or realistic. The simple truth is that I did not pack the right gear to achieve my business goal. However, I am extremely grateful, extremely fortunate, and I am extremely pleased with my accomplishments and have no regrets and am envious of no one.

We all would enjoy being both liked and respected. But if I must choose between being liked (going along with the crowd, being funny, having no convictions) or being respected (doing only that, which I know to be right, my word being accepted by others as a verbal contract) I will choose being respected every time.

I continually strive to be more of a realist and to be more pragmatic about myself, my abilities, and my appearance, rather than being egotistical. To prevent my ego from directing my thoughts and actions is always a struggle.

To be less judgmental about others.

ATTITUDE II

ATTITUDE

A positive attitude is the result of believing, you simply must believe.

I have never had a bad day in my life, some are just better than others.

I cannot be shown a situation in which I cannot find something positive within that situation. If nothing else I can say "could be worse."

The world cannot make you cry unless you let it.

Strive to do the best with the strengths and abilities that you have been given, for the simple truth is – we are what we are.

There is always light at the end of the tunnel, we just don't always know the length of the tunnel.

I am totally convinced that everything that happens in life is for the best. Sometimes it just takes a while to realize why.

The phrase "monitor the return on investment" is primarily related to business endeavors but the phrase also applies in one's personal life. Is the cost of fuel and the time and effort driving to get an ice cream cone worth the pleasure one receives from eating the ice cream cone. Being honest with one's self in regard to the return on investment will make one much happier.

Never be afraid to dream, but one must understand the difference between dreaming and wishing. To dream is to have a realistic goal and then to work very hard to achieve that goal. Attempting to be the first college graduate from one's family is a true dream. To wish is to hope for something that requires no effort. Winning the lottery and becoming rich is a true wish. Winners dream. Losers wish.

The wonderful ability that every human possesses is the ability to improve. No matter how well we have done, with effort and desire we can improve upon anything. However, we must be honest with ourselves and determine if improvement is necessary and is worth the effort. Is improvement in this instance a good return on investment?

Ever so often, one should look into the mirror and admit – I'm not the best, I'm not the prettiest or the smartest or the strongest – I'm not, nor ever will be the fastest gun in town (there will always be a faster gun) – and I could improve, but I'm not bad. It's perfectly all right to pat yourself on the back periodically. One should be very proud of their actions.

With a positive attitude one can overcome the majority of one's adversities in one's life. A serious health issue, such as the cancer I developed in 1995, requires several factors for a successful recovery. Acceptance of the situation, knowledge and expert advice to create and implement a plan of treatment, the love and support of others, and the desire to win and to go forward with one's life. Throughout the treatment process, the health issue should be considered as nothing more than a simple inconvenience in one's journey of life.

RIGHT AND WRONG III

RIGHT AND WRONG

By the time one has become an adult, a clear understanding of right and wrong has been established.

Listen to and trust your gut instincts. As one becomes older, the experiences one encounters will reinforce those gut feelings. You will find that in the vast majority of situations, your gut instinct will be correct in determining what is right and what is wrong.

Do only that, which you know to be right.

I always attempt to do only that, which I know to be right. I often fail, but I am forever trying.

I have two minds. One I call my right mind (doing only that, which I know to be right), the other I call my sissy mind (looking for the easy way). I am continually disappointed in how often my sissy mind overcomes my right mind.

13

The one time out of ten that you fail to do only that, which you know to be right – did not take your briefcase, did not make good notes, did not make that phone call, did not file the item properly, did not prepare, did not get the first and last name of the individual, etc., etc., etc., will also be the one time out of ten the right thing was necessary and the wrong thing was obvious. You got caught.

Doing the right thing is not always easy – but it is the right thing to do.

The ability to say the right thing at the right time is a wonderful characteristic but it requires a great deal of practice and effort.

Knowing what's right or wrong is important, but what really matters is knowing what is reality.

Reality is not always pretty.

The true litmus test of your behavior is being able to look at yourself in the mirror and to like what you see.

The first instance of doing something wrong or unethical or against one's sense of right or wrong (not declaring income from a part-time job on one's income tax report, taking office supplies from one's employer, missing a child's soccer game to play golf) is very difficult and requires a great deal of rationalization. The second instance the same activity occurs, doing something wrong or unethical or against one's sense of right or wrong is not quite as difficult and requires less rationalization. The third instance the same activity occurs, the instance is now considered by the individual to no longer be wrong and requires no rationalization.

When describing an individual to someone, use a defining feature that can in no way be considered insulting or demeaning. Never, ever use skin color or ethnicity to describe an individual.

Unfortunately we are all human beings and may occasionally have a thought about an individual or individuals that either is judgmental, racist, prejudicial, or cruel. We may not be able to prevent having the unfortunate thought, but we very definitely can prevent the terrible thought from coming out of our mouths. There simply is no excuse for saying something cruel.

Ethnic jokes should never be told.

WINNING AND LOSING IV

WINNING AND LOSING

At the end of the day we must determine whether we have won or lost the day. The positive element in the scoring is that we are our own score keeper.

In life there are only winners and losers. Losers always have an excuse that has nothing to do with their ineptitude. "It was too hot, I didn't have time, they didn't like me, the referee was against us, I was too tired, the sun got in my eyes" etc., etc., etc. They will also always include in their list of excuses, the battle cry of the loser "I did my best" or "I tried as hard as I could." On the other hand a winner will always admit a loss, (everyone loses once in a while as there are no perfect records in life). But a winner begins to immediately review what they did incorrectly and what can be done to improve their performance. They will regroup, regather their thoughts, redo their plan, revitalize their energy and interest, and win the next round. The battle cry of the winner is "I can and will do better."

A winner always loses with grace and dignity, walking away with their back straight and their head held high. There will always be another game and another day. Conversely, a winner always wins with grace and dignity, allowing their opponent to also maintain their grace and dignity. There is no valor in the total annihilation of one's opponent.

TELEVISION AND CELL PHONES V

TELEVISION AND CELL PHONES

Television is an easy way to eliminate boredom and should be used only as the last resort.

When a visitor comes into your home, the television should be turned off immediately unless the purpose of their visit is to watch a special program with you.

When you are in a public place, such as a restaurant, and are talking to someone, even if only a casual conversation, it is extremely rude and insensitive to glance at a television. It is also very noticeable.

A television does have an "off" switch, and it should be used frequently.

The invention of the cell phone has created a much more convenient means of communicating in both business and personal situations. The cell phone, when used properly, has eliminated a great many inconveniences and has made our lives, in some ways, simpler. Unfortunately the invention of the cell phone has also created a new set of discourteous behaviors. One should continue to be both courteous and attentive to others in all situations first and use one's cell phone second. One should seldom use a cell phone while shopping in a store. One should never use a cell phone while conducting a business transaction in a store, especially while checking out. One should not use a cell phone while walking for exercise. This is a perfect time to think, to enjoy the surroundings, or to visit with a friend or child. If one is in a meeting or visiting with someone, one should turn their cell phone off and allow the call to go to their voicemail. One should not play a game on their cell phone when talking to someone or entertaining at a party. When in the presence of another, use one's cell phone only if absolutely necessary and only when appropriate. When used properly and courteously, the cell phone is a wonderful invention.

ETHICS VI

ETHICS

The concept of always maintaining one's ethics and integrity in the conduct of both one's personal and business activities is not only right, but it is a true advantage in accomplishing one's personal and business goals.

Never engage in a verbal shoving match over something trivial. Your reputation and creditability are much too important. Unless your integrity or ethics are threatened, a verbal confrontation is not worth the effort.

If you must explain to an adult the meaning of pride, creditability, integrity, or ethics, they do not possess any of these traits or characteristics.

GIVING VII

GIVING

The perfect gift to give to someone is something they want or want to do but would never, ever buy or do for themselves. Never give to someone a personal item without asking them first. A good example is a watch. I have a watch that is perfect for me. I absolutely do not want any other watch of any type or of any cost. If someone were to give me a watch as a gift, regardless of the cost, it would create more harm than good. If I wear it, I am uncomfortable, if I don't wear it, the giver is uncomfortable. Some surprises are not good ideas or good gifts.

In regard to contributions and giving, I do not need a tax write-off to do what is right.

When someone asks if you can or will do something for them – your immediate response should be one thing and one thing only – "absolutely". Then ask what they are requesting and the details of the request. You may or may not be able to fulfill the request, but at least you have presented a positive attitude and an image of sincere interest.

One does not become a complete person until one begins to give to the less fortunate or to someone in need.

One should learn to give at a young age until giving from the heart, for the right reason, becomes a habit.

The best giver is a silent giver.

When one receives a gift, a gesture, or an expression of kindness, one should show appreciation of the gift or expression of kindness in one of several ways. A sincere thank you note is always appropriate, but also a subtle display of your appreciation is also very meaningful to the giver. In the case of clothing, try to wear the item in the presence of the giver or at least mention an event you attended while wearing the clothing. If an item, then display or use the item in the presence of the giver. If a compliment or a gesture, explain how much the compliment or expression of kindness meant to you or how you applied it in your daily life. Showing appreciation for a gift, even a bad gift, is worth the time, the effort, and the inconvenience. I have yet to read an article or hear about someone dying from wearing an ugly tie for a few moments or perhaps even a day, but I have heard many people speak of hurt feelings for not believing a gift, or an expression of kindness was appreciated. A giver deserves consideration and courtesy in all situations and never, ever rudeness or indifference.

Those that give regularly to the less fortunate or to someone in need will increase their success in all aspects of their business and personal life.

One must have a specific mission of giving in one's life.

PARENTING VIII

PARENTING

Being a parent becomes a worthwhile endeavor when a sincere compliment about a son or daughter is received by the parent. Nothing further is necessary.

A Grandparent's role is to be an encouraging fan in the grandstand of life, always watching, cheering, and applauding – but never, ever coaching. The parents are the coaches on the sideline of life, and the grandchild is the player in the game on the field of life. But the grandparent must always be ready, at a moment's notice, to be called out of the grandstand to assist the coaches with whatever needs they may request. The need may be financial – babysitting – errands – emotional support – general everyday help – emergencies of any type, and perhaps even on a rare occasion – advice. Once the requested assistance has been completed, the grandparent returns to the grandstand and again becomes an enthusiastic spectator.

The old adage that children finally grow up and realize how smart their parents have become is very true. However, at some point in time the parents will realize that their children have become more knowledgeable in some or possibly most aspects of life than themselves. Periodically the parents will find themselves actually seeking the advice of their children. The only advantage parents will then have is the experience of life. However, their children are now gaining that same experience day by day. Parents should be proud of this cycle, as the future of our society depends on children building and improving upon the efforts of their parents.

The home of parents should always be available and open to their children and grandchildren at anytime, day or night. Their children and grandchildren should be encouraged to come and go freely and to utilize the contents of the parent's home. The only regard is in using common sense and courtesy. Conversely, the home of the children and grandchildren is theirs and theirs only. The parents should never go to their children's or grandchildren's home unannounced or uninvited as their children and grandchildren have earned and deserve their privacy and independence.

OPINIONS AND SUGGESTIONS IX

OPINIONS AND SUGGESTIONS

When someone asks your opinion, you must quickly determine if that someone truly wants your opinion or suggestion or if they actually want a confirmation of their own opinion. You should respond accordingly.

Regardless of one's religious beliefs, attending a church will give one a much greater opportunity to associate with a better class of people.

When someone wants to tell you about a plan or idea or shows you something that they have done or have created, it is not always necessary to offer a suggestion on how to improve upon what they are telling or showing you. A compliment is the kindest and most appropriate response.

Every industry, except the one you are in, is a rip off.

Heavily tinted windows in a car are not only rude (what is the driver hiding from?), but they are also a safety issue. A good defensive driver needs to see what the other drivers are doing and where they are looking – heavily tinted car windows hinder good drivers from being good defensive drivers.

Do something everyday worth bragging about, even if it is to simply, not mess anything up.

A sandwich made by someone else is always better.

A man's identification is his profession or occupation. A woman's identification is her home, family, and neighborhood.

If men were meant to retire, there would be sport shows on television in the afternoon instead of Oprah Winfrey.

The deterioration of our society is a result of individuals not accepting responsibility and accountability for their own actions and the demise of the traditional family.

Standardization of efforts breeds productivity and productivity breeds profitability in your business life and goal attainment in your personal life.

Always adhere to the 7 P's. Prior Proper Planning Prevents Pathetically Poor Performance.

Opinions are like a person's rear end. Everyone has one and some of them smell. One should review their opinion for it's odor before revealing it in public.

When someone is speaking to you, let them finish without interrupting - do not walk on their words.

Never agree to a purchase before you know at least the approximate cost. If you do not ask first, then you have no one to blame but yourself if the cost is too much. If you did not ask first, you now must pay the amount without complaining.

Unfortunately in our society there are two standards of safety and courtesies for men and women. A man should always take great care to never cause a woman to feel uncomfortable or unsafe. In a parking lot, a man should always create a safe distance between an unaccompanied woman and himself, even if maintaining a safe distance is inconvenient. A man should always announce himself when approaching an unaccompanied woman to prevent startling her. When it is necessary for a man to come within a close proximity of a woman in a business environment, a man should always advise the woman of what he is doing and where he is. Suggestive, risqué, or vulgar language should never, ever be used in the presence of a woman (even if she does), unless the man knows her very, very, very well. A man should treat all women as he would wish his mother, his wife, his sister, his daughter, his granddaughter, or a close friend to be treated.

One should make every effort not to borrow items from others. When one does borrow an item, the five following situations can occur and only one situation is good:

1. Return item on time in good condition
2. Lose item
3. Break or damage item
4. Return item late
5. Forget to return item

When you borrow money from a friend or relative, that friend or relative will begin to watch and to question how you spend your money.

A man should not wear a cap or hat in a house, church, school, or office. It is acceptable for a man to wear a cap or hat in a store, mall, or hallway of an office building. A man should always remove his cap or hat when he is introduced to a woman. A man should always remove his cap or hat when a prayer is being said and when the national anthem is being played. A man should always remove his cap or hat when the flag of The United States of America is being honored. The removal of a man's cap or hat at the appropriate time is a traditional sign of respect.

KINDNESS AND BEHAVIOR X

KINDNESS AND BEHAVIOR

We hurt those that we love so easily, because we know we will be so easily forgiven.

We often brag about other people to other people, but we seldom brag to the person we are bragging about.

The proper response to a sincere compliment is a simple "thank you – what a nice thing to say – thank you." Nothing further is necessary or appropriate.

I seldom regret what I did – but I always regret what I didn't do.

I have never made a knee-jerk reaction that I didn't regret.

When one makes a glib comment to someone, one will either be considered funny and clever, or one will be considered rude and insensitive. There is no in between. I have regretted being glib on many occasions.

During the day, there are often subjects or topics or policies or ideas that I need to think about and resolve. If time is not available and if the thought process can be delayed, I place these items in my mental file cabinet and then when I am driving, or walking, or when I have a more convenient time, I will pull the items out of my mental file cabinet, think about them and make the necessary decision or plan.

Never make an important decision at night unless absolutely necessary. One's mind is always clearer and sharper in the morning.

One should always strive to be a better person than everyone else in regard to being sensitive to the feelings of others, being gracious, and in giving. The saying, "Do unto others as you would have them do unto you" is better stated – "Do unto others better than you would have them do unto you". When someone is nice to you, try to "out nice'em."

A wonderful trait and characteristic is the ability to listen very intently. Not only to others, but just as important is the ability to listen to what one's self is saying. I continue to amaze myself with some of the silly things I hear myself saying.

I believe that I have the emotions and sensitivities of the average person. Therefore I try to remember all actions or statements that were meant for me and how they affected me. If the action or statement affected me favorably, then I attempt to repeat that action or statement to someone else. If I determine that an action or statement hurt me in someway, even if only slightly, then I make every effort to never, ever repeat that action or statement to anyone to prevent hurting them in someway.

The bad things that a person does may amount to only ten percent of what that person attempts – unfortunately, that ten percent will normally overshadow the other ninety percent of the good things.

One should never burn a bridge behind them. One may have the need to recross that river someday.

One should never say never.

LIFE, SUCCESS, AND HAPPINESS XI

LIFE, SUCCESS, AND HAPPINESS

Regardless of his age, a man does not become totally self reliant until his father dies.

Life is a race with continual hurdles to jump and overcome – some are large and some are small – but they are always there. The last hurdle you overcome is truly the last step you will take, as there is no straight away in the race of life. The secret is to enjoy the time between the hurdles, and to always be ready for the challenge of the next hurdle.

You must make happiness happen. It requires effort.

There are no shortcuts to success.

I have had such a wonderful life and I am so extraordinarily fortunate, that I have no fear of dying. I consider each new day as icing on my cake of life, and I make every effort not to smear it. If for some reason I should lose everything, I ask only to be given the companionship of my lovely wife and the day shift at a convenience store within walking distance of our apartment.

When someone asks me "how's it going", I am hesitant to tell them how well it is really going. I am so fortunate that if I began to relate all the wonderful things that happen to me – I would sound like a braggart. People do not want to hear that much good news, so I simply say "it's going well, thanks for asking."

Please my lovely wife and you have pleased me.

One should always strive to be as grateful as one is fortunate.

Results are the proof of one's efforts.

The sewer of life is full of good intentions that have gone down the drain due to lack of effort.

OBSERVATIONS XII

OBSERVATIONS

A salesperson is the easiest person to sell to, as a salesperson always enjoys and respects a professional performance.

One's ability to express one's self in writing, utilizing proper grammar, proper punctuation, and correct spelling, is a definite display of one's intelligence.

Some old standards, traits, and characteristics never become old.

If one is bored, it is one's own fault.

Good judgment will overcome guilt.

A truly good friend knows how much money you make.

Silence is not uncomfortable with a truly good friend.

It is not a good sign when one knows an emergency room doctor or a funeral director by their first name.

The stages of a man realizing that he is aging: first he is older than policemen, next he is older than doctors, then he is older than ministers, and finally, all women, regardless of their age, address him as "sir".

If you should find yourself with someone and it is difficult to maintain a conversation due to a lack of conversational material, simply ask them about themselves. People enjoy talking about themselves, their family, or their work, and will do so with very little encouragement. However, do not expect them to ask about you – they seldom will

I prefer to hear about someone else rather than to talk about myself. Other people are much more interesting than I am and I always learn something from them. There are only a few people that I believe are truly interested in me and that can bring out the talk in me about me.

Just when I think I have seen or heard everything, I see or hear something new. Life's events continue to surprise me.

Some of the most enjoyable, insightful, and productive conversations I have had, both personal and business, were in the parking lot of a restaurant after having had lunch or dinner with someone. People feel less guarded and are more open when they have an easy and readily available escape route that the parking lot provides.

People are very protective about their family, close friends, and themselves. They may make a critical or derogatory statement about someone close to them or even about themselves, but they will become very defensive, insulted, or hurt if the same statement is made by someone else. I joke about being "an old man or senior citizen" but if someone else refers to me as "old", I find the statement to be insulting.

I enjoy sleeping and find it very difficult to get out of bed and start my day. Over the years I have learned that it is just as difficult to get out of bed at 4:00 AM, 5:00 AM, 6:00 AM, or even 10:00 AM, so I have also learned to force myself to get up as early as necessary and begin my day. When the alarm makes that irritating sound, I turn it off and immediately get out of bed. There is no advantage to sleeping any later.

The true benefit of a vacation is not to the employee, but to the employee's family. The employee must work much harder prior to the vacation to have the ability to be away. Then upon return from the vacation, the employee must work much harder to catch up and become current. It is very common for an employee to wonder after a vacation "why did I leave"?

One does not need to worry or be concerned about a workaholic. He or she is doing exactly what they enjoy. One should, however, be concerned and worry about the workaholic's family. They are the ones who are sacrificing.

The world would be a great place to live if it wasn't for the humans.

I truly hope that you have enjoyed my "Ramblings" and that perhaps you may have found some wisdom within them that you can and will apply to your everyday life.

Our life's journey can be so simple if we all would "Do only that, which we know to be right"!

May you always be a winner!